Hummingbirds

Hummingbirds

Melanie Votaw

COURAGE BOOKS

AN IMPRINT OF RUNNING PRESS
PHILADELPHIA • LONDON

FRONT COVER PHOTO AND BACK COVER PHOTO:
© Michael and Patricia Fogden

© 2007 by Running Press
All rights reserved under the Pan-American and International Copyright
Conventions
Printed in China

9   8   7   6   5   4   3   2   1
Digit on the right indicates the number of this printing

Library of Congress Control Number: 2006925839

ISBN 978-0-7624-2834-2

Photography research by Susan Oyama
Designed by Melissa Gerber
Written by Melanie Votaw
Edited by Jennifer Colella
Typography: Garamond, Bodoni Book, Kuenstler Script Black, Berthold
Script, Botanical MT, Woodtype Ornaments and Arabesque Ornaments.

This book may be ordered by mail from the publisher.
But try your bookstore first!

Published by Courage Books, an imprint of
Running Press Book Publishers
125 South Twenty-Second Street
Philadelphia, Pennsylvania 19103-4399

Visit us on the web!
www.runningpress.com

contents

Introduction

Hummingbirds, named for the humming sound of their lightning fast wings, have long captivated the imagination and wonder of onlookers, and for good reason. With over 340 known species, there are more different kinds of hummingbirds in the Americas than almost any other type of bird. Surprisingly adaptable, hummingbirds exist all the way from Alaska to the islands off the southern tip of South America, ranging in habitats as diverse as tropical forests, deserts, and the cold mountaintops of the Andes. Most of the United States and Canada boast beautiful hummingbirds, though nearly half of the known species live within ten degrees of the equator.

In addition to being incredibly widespread, hummingbirds are spectacularly diverse. Their sizes range from the bee hummingbird, which is tiny enough to perch on the eraser of a pencil, to a hummingbird nearly the size of a swift. They also come in a rainbow of colors, tail lengths, and bill shapes.

There's no question why this bird is called the snowcap hummingbird, as it hovers in the Costa Rican rainforest.

This Costa's hummingbird is a desert species common to the far southwest of the United States, though they winter just south of the Mexican border. They inhabit a very small geographic area, and development and loss of this habitat has put this bird on Audubon's WatchList. The white-breasted female is typically larger than the green-breasted, violet-crowned and throated male.

North and South America are the only continents that can lay claim to these amazing creations, as Asia, Africa, Australia, and Europe are all bereft of hummingbirds. In fact, when European explorers first visited the Americas and reported back to their home countries about a bird no larger than an insect, most early Europeans thought the stories to be made-up or mistaken. Not even Columbus's own hummingbird encounter written in his diaries could persuade Europeans to believe. It took many eye-witness accounts repeating the same incredible details before the hummingbird-less Europe was able to conceive of such an incredibly minute bird. Once the stories were believed to be true, humming-birds quickly captured the European imagination.

Of course, Europeans weren't the only ones enthralled by the uniqueness of the amazing bird. Indigenous peoples of North and South America have long admired and studied the hummingbird, and there are plenty of rich oral histories and stories from these cultures professing the magical origins and powers of the mysterious little creatures.

The fascination with these unusual birds has far from lessened over the years. With their beautiful colors, sleek and compact design, and acrobatic skill, the hummingbird is as fascinating to watch and study today as it has ever been. Gardeners and birdwatchers alike are learning more and more about how to live harmoniously with these special "hummers," as hummingbird enthusiasts like to call them. Together, human observation, science, and folklore have all given us a great understanding and appreciation for the true miracle of the hummingbird.

This colorful scintillant humming-bird looks resplendent as it probes nearby flowers for nectar.

The Miracle of Hummingbirds

Hummingbirds are a glowing example of nature's perfection. If they were any larger, they would not be able to hover, and if they were any smaller, they would not be able to eat enough to maintain their necessary high energy. Therefore, the greatest miracle about hummingbirds is that they manage to survive at all.

This green-breasted mango hovers over nectar-rich flowers at the famed La Selva Biological Station in Costa Rica. One of the most important sites for tropical rainforest research, La Selva is one of South America's premiere sites for scientists, birders, and conservationists. Established over thirty years ago, the site hosts over 400 bird species, including about 25 species of hummingbird.

A green hermit samples a poro flower in Costa Rica, showing off his iridescent, teal feathers and two long, white tail feathers.

Regarding size, hummingbirds are the smallest birds in the world, equivalent in size to a human thumb and weighing no more than a penny. In fact, some dragonflies are larger!

Of course, there's nothing belittling about the efficiency of a hummingbird's small size; in fact, they are actually able to do more with less. The hummingbird's heart beats eight times faster than the human heart and is proportionately larger than the heart of any other warm-blooded animal. Plus, the hummingbird's brain, while only the size of a pea, is comparatively larger than other birds' and provides a phenomenal memory and well-known intelligence.

Even with the smallest wingspan, hummingbirds manage to travel in the fast-lane, beating their wings an average of eighty times per second and capable of reaching two hundred wingbeats per second and over forty miles per hour. Most small birds have a wingbeat of less than thirty beats per second.

Minutest of the feathered kind,
Possessing every charm combined,
Nature, in forming thee, designed
That thou shouldest be,
A proof within how little space
She can comprise such perfect grace,
Rendering the lovely, fairy race
Beauty's epitome.

—Charlotte Smith

One of the **rarities**
of the country
and a little prodigy
of **nature**.

—Paul Le Jeune

To support their high energy and high productivity, the hummingbird is, by human standards, a confirmed sugar addict. They can drink the nectar from as many as three thousand flowers a day, eating every ten minutes, and consuming up to 75 percent of their body weight. If humans had this metabolism, you would have to eat twenty thousand calories daily—about fifty pounds of sugar or three hundred pounds of hamburger—just to maintain your weight.

It may seem ironic that the world's smallest bird is the one most preoccupied with food, but with the fastest metabolism of all vertebrates, a hummingbird could die within a day if it fails to take in more energy than it loses. Nectar is digested within an hour, and 97 percent of it is immediately converted into energy.

Feeding can be complicated with the curved beak of the white-tipped sicklebill, but some flowers, such as the heliconia pictured here, are able to accommodate it.

This male Anna's hummingbird has a metallic green back and an extended rose-red gorget along the sides of his neck and crown. The species is unique in that it is one of only two species to permanently live in the United States and Canada without migrating. They are also one of the few species to have at least a minimal bird song.

No sooner has the returned sun again introduced the vernal season, and caused millions of plants to expand their leaves and blossoms to the genial beams, than the little hummingbird is seen advancing on fairy wings, carefully visiting every opening flower cup.

—John James Audubon

Hummingbirds acquire nectar from flowers, and flowers require hummingbirds to pollinate them. Pollination is the process through which flowers reproduce, and any flower requiring a bird for pollination is called an "Ornithophilous," which literally means "bird lover." Essentially, every time a hummingbird sips nectar, the flower's anther brushes pollen onto the bird's body. When the bird probes its next dozen or so blossoms, the flowers' stigmas brush the pollen off the bird, allowing the plants to reproduce through this exchange of pollen.

In an amazing example of coevolution, hummingbird flowers have even adapted the location of their anthers so that they leave pollen on specific parts of the bird's body, ensuring that only the same type of flower will be properly positioned to collect the pollen. This prevents the specialized pollens from being wasted on the wrong flower.

The clover, said the hummingbird,
was fashioned for the bee,
but ne'er a flower, as I have heard,
was ever made for me.

❦

A passing zephyr paused, and stirred
some moonlit drops of dew
to earth; and for the hummingbird
the honeysuckle grew.

—Albert Bigelow Paine

There are a variety of pollinators that help flowers to reproduce, including bees, moths, and bats. Evolution has helped to decrease competition and reproduce as many flowers as possible by providing each pollinator with a perfectly suited flower. In the case of hummingbirds, competition is also reduced by the feeding preferences of hummingbird species. Some hummingbirds will only feed at one elevation or level of the canopy, some feeding only from one kind of flower, while others feed more buffet style. These differences keep competition to a minimum.

Flowers and Pollinators

Flowers pollinated by insects are typically blue, smell sweet, have high concentrations of sugar, and must have a perch for the insect to use for landings.

Flowers pollinated by bats or moths are typically white and smell sweet so nocturnal animals can locate them in the dark.

Hummingbird flowers are vividly colored, usually tubular-shaped, and have no scent—perfect since hummingbirds have great eyesight but no sense of smell.

An Anna's hummingbird hovers beside a flower. This bird does not have a distinctive red gorget, which means it is either an adolescent male or a female.

A male tufted coquette perches on a vine and tastes the air with his long tongue. He is a very small hummingbird, measuring only 2 ¾ inches from beak to tail, and inhabits areas of South America. He is popular amongst bird watchers because of his vibrant red feathers and "punk rock" head feathers and neck tufts.

One of the major adaptations that evolution has used to differentiate pollinators and their flowers is the hummer's long, tapered bill, which is perfectly suited to tubular flowers that are too deep for other pollinators. These bills are made of a material similar to the horn of an antelope and are generally brown or black in color, although some species sport red bills. Bill sizes and shapes vary from species to species, causing them to specialize in certain flowers, which is another measure to reduce competition for food.

The hummer's tongue is also essential in feeding. It has approximately fifty taste buds along its length, is translucent, and somewhat stretchy. It can extend beyond the length of the bill to lick nectar at the ravenous pace of twelve licks or more per second.

> . . . *He* sucks his Food, the Honey Dew,
> With nimble Tongue, and Beak of jetty Hue. . . .
> And as he moves his ever-flutt'ring Wings,
> Ten thousand Colours he around him flings. . . .
> Thus whirring round he flies, and varying still
> He mocks the *Poet's* and the *Painter's* Skill. . . .
>
> —Richard Lewis

Desert hummingbirds manage to find plenty of food in their environment. For example, this parasitic flower living on an eulychnia cactus provides nectar for hummers.

In addition to all of the nectar that hummingbird adaptations make it possible to eat, hummingbirds also need protein, which they get by consuming insects. One hummer can partake of more than six hundred insects in a single day, digesting them in ten minutes. Hummingbirds will consume any insect small enough to swallow, including ants, caterpillars, mosquitoes, gnats, aphids, fruit flies, and larvae. Sometimes, hummingbirds will "hawk" the insects mid-flight, or they might "glean" the insects by picking them off plants, trees, or even purposely turning over leaves to expose insects underneath.

Art thou a bird, a bee, or butterfly?
Each and all three—a bird in shape am I,
A bee collecting sweets from bloom to bloom,
A butterfly in brilliancy of plume.

—James Montgomery

The brilliant colors of the velvet-purple coronet include glistening blues, greens, purples, yellows, and oranges, making them one of the most colorful hummingbird species. This particular coronet flies straight toward long, tubular, red blossoms, an ideal and favored hummingbird flower. Most velvet-purple coronets live in tropics or subtropics, especially in Ecuador and Columbia, and they prefer wet, marshy woods or the borders of forests.

The most remarkable
group of birds in
the entire world.

—Robert Ridgway

These calliope hummingbirds are found throughout the United States and Canada, though they winter in Mexico. They are most often found in high mountains and like to nest near water sources. Females have white-tipped tail feathers, a green back, and buff sides, whereas the male has a green back, white gorget, and whiskered purple streaks.

The hummingbird feeding frenzy of nectar and insects begins at dawn. After waking, the bird will need to eat right away in order to make up for the energy lost during the night. A hummingbird will spend the majority of its day at rest, but only for short periods of time as it digests, preens, and perches by food sources. Feeding will take place up to fifteen times per hour during the day.

At dusk, the hummingbird gorges itself in order to store enough energy to make it through the night without feeding. Without this energy storage, it would die of hypothermia, making sleep a dangerous undertaking. If the night is warm and there has been plenty of food to eat, the bird will be able to sleep normally.

If the night has been cold or food has been too scarce to store enough energy, the bird will go into a coma-like state called torpor, which is similar to hibernation. The lower a hummingbird's body temperature can safely go during the night, the less energy it will expend. In the torpid state, minutes may pass without a single breath, and the bird will appear to be dead. People have lifted a supposedly dead hummingbird from a branch only to find it awakening and flying away a few hours later. This hibernation can be dangerous, as illness, predators, or excessive cold can cause hummers to perish during this sort of sleep, but it allows hummingbirds to survive in cold altitudes.

In the Torpid State

- The hummingbird's normal 105 degree Fahrenheit body temperature can drop below 50 degrees.

- The heart rate can slow to less than forty beats per minute from the average thousand beats per minute during the day.

- It can take less than an hour to enter torpor, but it takes awhile to wake up from, as the body temperature needs to be 86 degrees Fahrenheit for flight.

- Torpor can be maintained for as long as fourteen hours.

While all hummingbirds must budget their energy and slow their metabolism at times, tropical hummingbirds, such as this blue-chinned sapphire found mostly in South America, don't have to worry as much about torpor as those birds in higher altitudes and colder climates. So long as these birds are able to gorge before sleep, they can rest normally in the temperate evening.

Given the serious repercussions for not finding enough food, hummingbirds are fiercely territorial to protect and watch over food sources. While hummers can sometimes be shy, their speed and unmatched agility make them virtually fearless, ready and willing to take on any adversary that gets in their way, from tiny insect to giant human. Hummingbirds will kick their claws out in mid-flight, dive-bomb another, or lock bills and circle to the ground. Hummingbirds rarely hurt other hummingbirds in these bouts, but one bird may win the territory of another.

Putting up a Fight

- Before resorting to combat, hummingbirds will try to deter intruders with vocalized warnings and chases.

- Fight behavior appears to be instinctive, as chicks begin showing aggression just days after leaving the nest.

- Hummingbirds have even been known to successfully chase away birds as large as hawks and other potential predators.

The male coppery-headed emerald demonstrates the territorial nature of all hummingbirds as he tries to drive another hummingbird away from a prized food source. Whether a larger adversary or from the same species, the hummingbird is uncompromising when it comes to nectar.

These two green-crowned brilliants may look
like they are sharing a branch, but they are
probably either vying for territory and food
or courting one another.

The constant competition and territoriality necessitates a solitary life, which makes mating difficult. The female usually begins the courtship process by approaching the male's feeding territory, and he will chase her into a neutral area where he will perform courtship displays and attempt to impress her. These courtship rituals can be very entertaining and are often indistinguishable from fighting displays.

Each species has unique courtship behaviors, though many general dances and movements are shared amongst most hummingbirds. For example, a Peruvian species has the unique habit of raising the round circles on the end of his tail feathers around his face, whereas the Anna's hummingbird has the more common practice of flying high above the female and then swooping down toward her.

Males will have plenty of opportunities to practice their dance, as they will mate as often as possible and attempt to impress as many females as they can. On the other hand, females typically only mate one to two times per season. Both will enter into this crazy dating game at about one year old.

Some Courtship Dances

- U-, J-, or O-shaped dives from an elevated height down toward the female.

- Whistling, snaps of the tail, song, or other sounds.

- "Shuttle flights," or a swooping from side to side like a hypnotist's watch.

- Using the feathers to highlight the face or body.

Dance and flight aren't everything that a male will need to impress a female in a courtship. Song is also occasionally used in the courtship dance, and hummingbirds do indeed sing, although they are hardly the most melodic members of the avian world. Lacking the strong vocal muscles of songbirds, the number of calls and songs that a hummingbird can perform differ from species to species. Some have beautiful and varied songs, while other species chant a single note. However, given their beauty and spectacular assets in other areas, it hardly seems fair to expect hummingbirds to also be expert singers.

The Ruby-throat needs no song.
Its beauty gives it distinction,
and its wings make music.

—Frank M. Chapman

The exception to this general rule is the famous singing hummingbird species, the less colorful hermit hummingbird. This tropical species will congregate in groups, called *leks*, with up to a hundred males and sing to attract females. Other species, such as manakins, also create leks for this purpose. These choirs will sing the same song up to twelve thousand times per day for nine months of the year.

The long-billed starthroat flies near desired flowers in South America. The species is widespread in the tropics and spans into several countries.

This Costa's hummingbird perches on a flower and shows off his deep-blue gorget and iridescent side and back feathers. With a simple flick of his head, his feathers could appear drab and plain, which allows males to catch the eye of interested females in courtship without catching the attention of larger predators.

Feathers are also essential in courtship and for everyday flight. Hummingbird feathers are beautiful and glisten iridescently in sunlight. The males of most species are especially vibrant and sport colors that can suddenly change with the direction of the sun. The male throat and chin, called the gorget, is the area that most often changes color, suddenly blazing with the intensity of a flashlight. Males are very aware of these colors and know how to flash color to attract a female and how to appear colorless to escape predators. The females tend to be less colorful, which helps them avoid predators while nesting.

Feathers radiate this color by using a technical process called interference, which is similar to that which creates a rainbow in a soap bubble. Feathers are made of microscopic "barbules," which reflect as mirrors. When stacked together, barbules make color and iridescence especially intense. The direction in which barbules reflect light also determines a hummingbird's angle of iridescence.

Why do I **wonder** how you would look in hummingbird feathers?

—Carl Sandburg

In addition to looking beautiful and impressing females, feathers are strong, light, waterproof, and insulating. The hummingbird also has more feathers per square inch of skin than any other bird, making them an essential survival feature for the hummingbird.

> There is no easy way to bathe a hummingbird.
>
> —Kehlog Albran

Because feathers are so important, keeping them in optimal condition is essential. Bathing is a crucial job that must be done several times a day. A birdbath or any small pool of standing water will suffice, though showers are preferable. Preening is also important. Both the bill and claw perform this task expertly by extracting oil from a gland near the tail and combing it through feathers. This oil is much like a waxy polish that keeps feathers beautiful, properly placed, and removes dust and mites. Keeping feathers in good shape ensures survival and helps with wooing a female hummingbird during courtship.

Like a multi-faceted rainbow, properly groomed hummingbird feathers catch the sunlight and glimmer in several brilliant colors.

Hummingbird Nests

- Building a nest can take up to two weeks.
- Most hummingbird nests are smaller than a baseball, with some barely large enough to hold a nickel.
- Nests are often camouflaged into their habitat.
- North American species build cup-shaped nests, but some South American hummingbirds build hanging nests.

These black-chinned hummingbirds rest in their well-constructed, cup-shaped nest.

After being selected by a female and mating, the male will return to his territory and take no further part in raising the chicks. The female, who builds a nest prior to seeking a mate, will lay about two eggs. Females use whatever materials are available in the habitat to construct a nest, which can include lichens, bark, moss, leaves, fur, feathers, caterpillar silk, and even cloth or dryer lint. Spider web silk is frequently used to hold it all together like glue. Of course, comfort also counts for something when building a home. The female knows this and takes care to make the outside sturdy and firm with an insulated, cushiony interior. In some locations, nests are even constructed with roofs, counterweights, or other additions to guarantee safety.

Nest building and mating, unsurprisingly, happen when the most flowers are in bloom, often in early spring for some species. Migrating birds begin building nests and courting one another as soon as they arrive in their summer habitat. The female especially will want to mate while flowers are bountiful so she will have an easier time feeding herself and the chicks.

While some cup-shaped nests are slightly elongated to stay safe and secure on shaky branches, this one is perfectly round and holds a snow-white egg and newly born chick.

Laid safely in the nest, eggs are about half the size of a jelly-bean and amount to almost 20 percent of the female's weight. The mother will carefully incubate the eggs for a little over two weeks to maintain the eggs' temperature.

At this point, the chicks break out of their eggs with the help of a temporary tooth on their bills. They are born blind, have no feathers, and are silent. Their mother will feed them three times per hour with nectar and insect mixtures until they can feed themselves. Their eyes won't open until their second week, and by their fourth week, most species' chicks are ready to take their first flight and set out on their own. Only 60 percent of chicks live long enough to make their first flight, but those who do generally live to be three to five years old.

The woods hold not such another
gem as the nest of the hummingbird.
The finding of one is an event.

—John Burroughs

Adaptations for Flight

🐾 Hummingbirds, unlike other birds, have short arm bones, long finger bones, and flex only at the shoulder.

🐾 Hovering is possible because of the ability to rotate wings *both* vertically and horizontally, allowing for a rapid figure-eight movement.

🐾 A deep sternum, two extra ribs, and strong chest muscles help to attain lift on *both* up and downward wingbeats, which other birds can't do.

🐾 Hummingbirds have nine air sacs in the lungs instead of the regular six, which provides continuous air and energy for difficult air maneuvers.

🐾 As with all flying birds, bones are hollow and weigh two to three times less than their feathers.

What heavenly tints in mingling radiance fly!
Each rapid movement gives a different dye;
Like scales of burnished gold they dazzling show,
Now sink to shade, now like a furnace glow!

—Alexander Wilson

After achieving this first flight, the hummingbird will be capable of dramatic and daring aerial feats made possible by their unique anatomy—even our most impressive *Top Gun* maneuvers fail to come close.

A quick tilt of the wings, and hummingbirds can change direction in an instant. They are the only birds that can fly in all directions, including sideways, backward, and upside-down. However, it's their ability to constantly hover that fascinates us most, as other small birds can hardly do it at all. Hummingbirds have a true command of the air unparalleled in the avian world.

Graceful, poised, and elegant, all hummingbirds can hover below, above, or beside blossoms, and they have no need for perches.

Perhaps the greatest feat of hummingbird flight isn't the impressive tricks, but the long distances hummingbirds migrate each season. To prepare for migration, hummingbirds will gorge for several days to almost double their weight. The storage of body fat allows the birds to fly as high as ten thousand feet and up to five hundred miles at a time, even through the night without eating or sleeping. Sometimes, they fly until their energy is almost depleted, making periodic stops to replenish their storage. The majority of species in South America do not migrate, as their habitats offer a temperate climate year round. On the other hand, Anna's and Allen's hummingbirds are the only two species in North America that do not migrate.

Rufous hummingbirds are unique in that they can migrate the longest distances and out-fly all other hummingbirds, though they must gorge before such feats.

Long Distance Migration

- Over five billion hummingbirds migrate every year.

- Ruby-throated hummingbirds travel up to 2,000 miles per year, and the rufous hummingbird will fly 2,500 miles per season from Mexico to Alaska.

- Hummingbirds do not flock, but rather migrate alone.

- Juvenile hummers are not taught which direction or route to fly by other hummers, so they must use an internal navigation system.

- It's believed that hormone changes triggered by changing daylight hours will tell a hummingbird when to migrate for the season.

Hummingbirds in Our Midst

It can be an extraordinary experience to begin watching and studying the hummingbird. If you live in the Americas, there are probably hummingbirds in your area, and there are a variety of ways to attract them and bring these wonderful birds into your life. It can take two seasons before the hummingbirds begin to visit your food sources regularly, but it's well worth the time. If you live in the city, have no backyard, or have no hummers in the area, there are still plenty of options for hummingbird close-encounters.

This young ruby-throated hummingbird perches on a fence in Rock Creek Park, Washington, DC. The ruby-throated hummingbird is one of the most popular hummingbirds found in the eastern United States. Parks can be great places to try and observe a couple of hummers.

I hear like you see—like that
hummingbird outside that
window for instance.

—Ray Charles

*This Anna's hummingbird keeps
its feathers in tip-top shape with a
refreshing dip in a nearby fountain.*

The first step to attracting hummingbirds is to check with your local Audubon Society or other birding groups to see if you have hummers in your area, especially if you live in a plain, marshland, shoreline, or mountain habitat.

If you have no hummingbirds frequenting your location, consider taking a birdwatching trip. The Sonora Desert of Arizona is the ultimate in North American hummingbird watching, though Texas and Louisiana are also great hummingbird locations. For exotic hummers, consider Ecuador and Columbia to see the most variety, or Costa Rica, Trinidad, Venezuela, Panama, and Brazil, which also have great birding sites. A search on the Internet will yield infinite choices regarding locations, ecolodges, and tours designed specifically for birders.

Always in the air, flying from flower to flower, it shares their freshness and their splendor, lives on their nectar and only inhabits those climates in which they are unceasingly renewed.

—Georges-Louis le Clerc de Buffon

If you have hummers in the area, consider if you are willing to acquire the needed materials and put in the required effort for gardening or feeder maintenance, and check to make sure that you have room for a feeder or a garden. If one of these elements is lacking, any local birding group can recommend nearby bird sanctuaries, zoos, and parks that attract hummingbirds, which will allow you to visit and see hummers without worrying about the time or space necessary with gardens and feeders. The only equipment necessary for bird-watching in these locations will be a set of good binoculars.

Feeders, like this red one, are a great way to attract hummers to your home. This violet-crowned hummingbird is particularly happy with the feeder it found. This species is most common in the southern and western part of the United States, though they winter in Mexico.

All hummingbirds, including this striking purple-throated mountain-gem, are attracted to beautiful flower blossoms.

If you want to attract hummingbirds to your backyard, the perfect hummingbird experience, of course, is the natural garden. Just a few of the trees and plants preferred by hummingbirds are: azalea, begonia, bromeliads, butterfly bush, cannas, cardinal flower, columbine, coral bells, cosmos, crab apple, delphinium, foxglove, fuchsia, geranium, hollyhocks, honeysuckle, impatiens, Indian paintbrush, lilac, lily, monkeyflower, morning glory, nasturtium, redbud, rose of Sharon, tree tobacco, and wisteria. Check with your local nursery to find out which plants will best grow in your region.

> Those who call it the flower-bird would, in my opinion, speak more correctly if they would call it the flower of birds.

—Paul Le Jeune

Gardening Considerations

❦ Plant flowers that bloom at different times of the year.

❦ Place gardens where they will be protected from excessive wind.

❦ Keep your garden away from hornets' nests, as they can hurt hummingbirds and their chicks.

❦ Never use pesticides in a hummingbird garden.

Feeders can be a great complement to gardens. There are upside-down bottle feeders and saucer-shaped feeders. Either will work, though with saucer feeders, try to get one with a roof to prevent rain from diluting the mixture. Red is a common feeder color, but it isn't absolutely necessary. Yellow feeders may attract bees or wasps.

It is necessary to clean hummingbird feeders every 3–4 days, more if the weather is unusually warm where you live, to avoid the growth of deadly fungi. Empty the feeder and flush with hot water. If it requires more cleaning, use a mixture of water and vinegar, but never soap. If black mold is present, you may soak the feeder in mild bleach water—be sure to rinse repeatedly, remove all of the bleach, and allow it to air dry. Have feeders back up every morning by dawn, or you run the risk of losing your hummingbirds.

Feeding from epiphytic heath in the cloudforest of Costa Rica, this male purple-throated mountain-gem displays his brilliant purple gorget. As his name suggests, this species is found mostly in hilly terrain and the mountains of Costa Rica, Nicaragua, and Panama. These birds tend to be aggressive and generally achieve dominance over other hummingbirds that may enter their area.

Other Considerations for Feeders

- If there's competition for feeders between hummingbirds or other nectar-feeding animals, put up several feeders with and without perches.

- Make sure feeders are shielded from wind and that objects are nearby for perching.

- Hummingbird flowers nearby will help, or place overripe fruit in a secluded area to attract fruit flies, which will also attract hummingbirds.

- Keep your distance until the birds become accustomed to you.

- If your feeder is near the window, attach decorations to prevent hummingbirds from flying into or attacking the window.

- Do not place feeders where cats roam freely. If you own an outdoor cat, consider not putting up feeders.

Now, how do you make sugar water for feeders? It's very easy, and while there are commercial solutions for sale, they are no better than your own solution and may actually spoil more quickly. Simply mix four parts water to one part white cane sugar. *Never* use brown sugar, sugar substitute, or honey, as it's dangerous to birds.

Always boil the water (add extra for the water that boils away), and then add four parts water to one part sugar (for example: mix ¼ cup sugar with 1 cup water). Allow the mix to cool completely before filling the feeder. If needed, sugar water will keep for a few days in the refrigerator. *Never* increase the amount of sugar in your homemade nectar, as hummingbirds dislike it and it may cause harm, and *never* add red food coloring to nectar. Distilled water is also not recommended.

. . . I this very past summer planted some sunflowers to thrust their great disks out from the hollow and allure the bee and the hummingbird.

—Nathaniel Hawthorne

This red sugar-water feeder in Arizona offers extra energy, nutrients, and easy feeding to visiting hummingbirds.

The sugar water in your feeders will attract other types of insects and animals. Some of the newer feeders are equipped with moats or guards that prevent insects from reaching the nectar, but do not attempt to use oil or duct tape around feeders to discourage insects, as it harms hummingbirds. Bats are also nectar eaters and may raid your feeders during the night. Bear in mind that these animals also pollinate many plants, so think twice before denying them nectar. The problem is that bats could leave the feeders empty by dawn when the hummers arrive, but if you're an early riser, you have the option of feeding both kinds of animals.

The buff-bellied male and female hummingbirds are found mostly south of Texas. They are relatively large with green coloring and buff bellies.

He never stops, but slackens

Above the Ripest Rose—

Partakes without alighting

And praises as he goes,

Till every spice is tasted . . .

—Emily Dickinson

This broad-tailed hummingbird summers in the south and west of the United States, but it winters in Mexico.

Have you ever observed a hummingbird moving about in an aerial dance among the flowers—a living prismatic gem. . . . In its exquisite form, its changeful splendour, its swift motions and intervals of aerial suspension, it is a creature of such fairy-like loveliness as to mock all description.

—W. H. Hudson

If your feeders have been up for a couple of weeks and no birds are visiting, try hanging red ribbon from them, or add orange or red tape on the feeder where the birds do not perch. Bear in mind that if the birds frequenting your yard are unfamiliar with the type of feeder hanging there, it may take them a few days to try it. Plus, there may be fewer birds during the summer months when the females are nesting. With time, your back-yard will become an established territory, and you can expect migratory species to visit you every summer. You might even have hummers visiting in the winter, as it is recommended that you leave feeders up all winter if the nectar doesn't run the risk of freezing. Winter feeders can be a lifeline for birds too young or too slim to migrate.

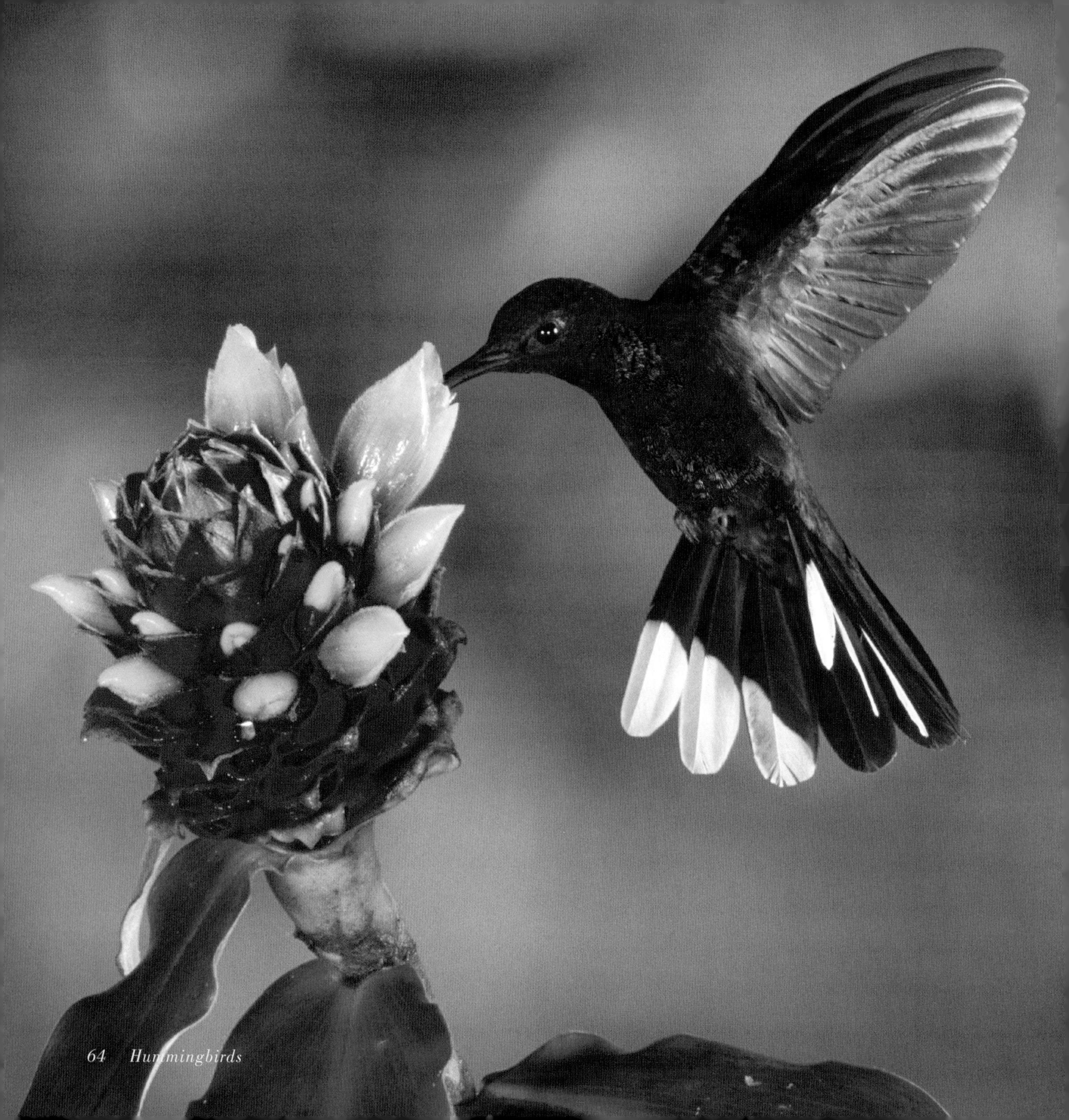

> Now here, now there, thy flash is seen, like some stray sunbeam darting, with scarce a second's space between its coming and departing.

—George Murray

This male violet sabrewing shines with color and shows off his white, outer tail feathers as he hovers at a ginger flower in a cloudforest of Costa Rica. He is one of the larger hummingbirds and has been pictured on the stamps of several Central American countries. Like the hermits, the males of this species sing together in leks.

Once birds start visiting, you will have opportunities for hummingbird photography. If interested, you will need more than a point and shoot camera. It's recommended that you buy a 35 mm single lens reflex camera or advanced digital camera with a high quality lens and a manually-set shutter speed. A lens that can reach at least 300 mm is preferable. High-speed film and flash attachments can help, but high-speed films tend to produce grainier prints and cannot be enlarged without loss of quality. Also, be aware of the position of lighting and your background. If taking photos through a window, be sure to press the lens directly against the glass to reduce flash.

If you take the time to learn as much as you can about photography in general and your equipment specifically, you should eventually get some beautiful photos.

I may not feel:
—I never may behold
The spark of life, that
trimmed in garb so bright
That flying quintessence of
ruby, gold, mild emerald,
and lucid chrysolite . . .

—Hartley Coleridge

Once you become accustomed to hummingbirds in your yard, you will be in a position to notice if a bird is in need of help or care of some kind. For example, you may discover a hummingbird wintering in a very cold environment, a bird that seems to be injured or ill, or abandoned chicks. Before calling the authorities, keep in mind that hummingbirds go into torpor, chicks may lie on the ground while learning to fly, and a mother can be away from her nest for up to thirty minutes. Without getting too close, watch and see if the situation improves.

If assistance is needed, call your local Audubon Society or wildlife rescue agency. If there are no local agencies, check online directories with the International Wildlife Rehabilitation Counsel or the National Wildlife Rehabilitation Association. Never touch or handle a wild bird yourself—it's dangerous, illegal, and you could do more harm than good.

This female broad-tailed hummingbird normally summers in the south and western United States, and it also enjoys Mexico's warmer winter climates. Unlike the adult males that sport a brilliant, red gorget, the female and young males have snowy-white throats.

A hummingbird we knew him
to be at once . . . a hummingbird in
adversity . . . Immediately, however,
we sent out to have him taken in.

—Harriet Beecher Stowe

*Found mostly in Venezuela and Trinidad
and Tobago, the copper-rumped hummingbird
is one of many beautiful species that can only
be seen in South America.*

Helping to keep hummers alive and safe is very important, as some of the exotic species you may see while birding abroad may include one of about seventy species in danger of extinction. Because of their remarkable speed and flying ability, adult hummingbirds are rarely caught by natural predators. Snakes, spiders, cats, praying mantises, larger birds, and some other animals will occasionally capture a hummingbird, and migration and severe weather can also be dangerous.

However, like most animals in the Americas, urban sprawl and rainforest deforestation are the worst threat, already believed to have eliminated entire species. Hummingbirds rely on their memory of lush, nectar-rich habitats to guide them, and when they fly to a location and find changed landscapes, they could die of starvation within a day while searching for new nectar locations. This is one reason why feeders, hummingbird gardens, and conservation are so important.

Hummingbirds
in History and
Folklore

ittle is known about how hummingbirds evolved through the ages. Because of their small size, no fossils remain to determine how long they have survived on the planet. Some scientists believe they began in the northern Andes of South America, while others theorize they evolved in the tropics and moved north. Scientists agree, however, that their wide range of habitat indicates they have been in existence for a long time, and they have inspired stories, cultures, and science since man first discovered the little avian wonder.

This rufous-tailed hummingbird is very territorial and dominant over most other hummingbirds. Their area is relatively small, living mostly in South American countries, compared with the rufous hummingbird, which can be anywhere from Mexico to Alaska.

And the hummingbird that hung
like a jewel up among
the tilted honeysuckle-horns,
they mesmerized and swung
in the palpitating air,
drowsed with odors strange and rare,
and with whispered laughter, slipped away,
and left him hanging there.

—James Whitcomb Riley

With beautiful colors and unsurpassed aerial grace, hummingbirds have served as muses for a variety of poets, writers, and storytellers. From Richard Lewis in the 17th century to W. H. Hudson in the 20th, the minute bird has managed to fly its way into the pages of literature and history thanks to some of its very famous and talented admirers. A few of these fan-club members include D. H. Lawrence, Harriet Beecher Stowe, Nathaniel Hawthorne, and Emily Dickinson, though even army officers, priests, farmers, actors, and naturalists have sung and written their praises throughout the ages.

With glittering greens and pretty pinks, this hummer has plenty of color to go around, except on its belly. Known as the snowy-bellied hummingbird for this obvious reason, the bird proudly shows vibrant colors as it prepares for take-off.

Purple-throated mountain-gems, like all hummingbirds, have feet, though it's easy to see why so many people believe they don't. The tiny feet are so small that hummingbirds must rely on their wings to move, walk, and turn. The feet are used mostly for perching.

That humankind has long been enamored with hummingbirds is obvious in the poetic names given to the various species, such as "brilliant," "emerald," "comet," "sunangel," "mango," "coquette," "starfrontlet," and "mountain-gem."

Attempting to get away from the poetic names and establish scientific categories, Linnaeus was the first to publish biological data on hummingbirds, although science of the 1750s did not afford him total accuracy. He believed hummingbirds had no feet, which is why he named their avian order in biology "Apodiformes," the prefix of which translates to "without feet."

What dainty epithets thy tribes
Have won from men of science!
Pedantic and poetic scribes
For once are in alliance.

—George Murray

Half bird, half fly, the fairy king of flowers
Reigns there, and revels through the fragrant hours;
Gem full of life and joy and song divine!

—Samuel Rogers

Despite scientific findings, Native American legends in both North and South America have their own thoughts on the origin and order of hummingbirds. Mayan legend says that the hummingbird was the last bird created. Because it was made from leftover, drab feathers, the other birds felt sorry for it and gave it some of their most beautiful parts. The resplendent quetzal offered its iridescent green feathers, the house finch donated its red gorget, and the swallow gave its white tail feathers. The hummingbird of Mayan culture, made colorful by the generosity of other birds, became associated with the sun, which disguised itself as the beautiful bird in order to seduce the moon.

Looking bejeweled in gems and sparkles, this crowned woodnymph from Costa Rica has beautiful contrasts between its drab body and iridescent plumage. It's easy to see why the hummingbird's unique beauty inspired so many myths.

In a display of just how different hummingbirds can be, the long-tailed hermit hummingbird tends to be more romantic, though less colorful, than other hummingbirds. The males of the species are less aggressive territorially than seen in other hummers, which allows them to congregate in leks. In these groups, males attempt to woo females with song and courtship dances.

Many tribes share an association of the hummingbird with seduction and love. Its feathers have been used for generations to make love charms and are said to open the heart. Ancient Mexicans wore stuffed hummingbirds around their necks to inspire affection and even ground the dried heart of the bird into an aphrodisiac. The Jatibonicu Taino tribe of Puerto Rico even paint the hummer and its love of flowers as a forbidden, star-crossed love. According to the legend, a young man and woman from rival tribes fell in love, but their families disapproved. To escape the criticism and to be together forever, one of the pair became a hummingbird; the other became a red flower.

Quick as a hummingbird is my love,
Dipping into the hearts of flowers—
She darts so eagerly, swiftly, sweetly,
Dipping into the flowers of my heart.

—James Oppenheim

Even more associated with magical properties, the Aztecs of Central America named their gods after hummingbirds and adorned themselves with hummingbird feathers, which they believed could remove curses. The Aztecs also believed that the first flower came into being when the god of music and poetry disguised himself as a hummingbird and romanced a goddess in the underworld. Obviously, the Aztecs held the hummingbird in very high regard, even giving the small bird, or at least a god taking the form of the bird, credit for leading them to the rich and fertile island on which they built their civilization. Within this culture, the powers of the hummingbird were very diverse and at least partly responsible for the creation and success of their kingdom.

A flash of harmless lightning,
A mist of rainbow dyes,
The burnished sunbeams brightening
From flower to flower he flies.

—John Banister Tabb

This little hermit hummingbird feeds from tubular, yellow flowers with its long beak. With the exchange of pollination that will take place through the feeding, the hummingbird will help create new blossoms in new areas and plants.

A violet sabrewing is a long-beaked bird with a dark-green back and violet front. This one fans his white-tipped tail as he hovers at the yellow flowers of justice in Costa Rica. His long, slightly curved bill is well suited for these flowers.

A multitude of people and tribes give the hummingbird credit for helping to create the world and its beauty. In addition to the Aztec's guiding hummingbird, the Jatibonicu Taino believe that it is the hummingbird's mission to bring new life to earth through the flower blossom. The Mojave give the hummingbird more responsibility and tell the story of a time when people lived under the ground and knew only darkness. It was the hummingbird that flew from the darkness to the land of the sun, and he led the people to the lighted world. The Ohlone of California believe the hummingbird was actually one of three creators of the world, standing beside Eagle and Coyote when the world was only water.

Before anything had a soul,

While life was a heave of matter, half inanimate. . . .

I believe there were no flowers then,

In the world where the hummingbird flashed ahead of creation.

I believe he pierced the slow vegetable veins with his long beak.

—D.H. Lawrence

Other tribes associate the hummingbird more fully with death. This is unsurprising given the hummingbird's ability to enter a death-like state in torpor, and it has created a lot of ties to the underworld, healing, and spirits. The Chayma people of Trinidad would never harm a hummingbird, as the birds are believed to be the spirits of their ancestors. The Pueblo use hummingbird feathers to speed reincarnation, to give new life just as the hummingbird comes out of torpor with new life. Hummers are also said to have general healing powers and have been called "doctor birds." According to Mayan legend, hummingbirds could even call forth a person's ancient ancestors through a blood ritual. The main reason for these supposed powers is the old belief that the hummer died every autumn, went to the underworld, and was reborn every spring.

Hummingbirds . . . most elegantly finished in all parts, it is a miniature work of our Great Parent—who seems to have formed it the smallest, and at the same time the most beautiful, of the winged species.

—Hector St. John de Crevecoeur

Preparing to swoop in on the red, nectar-filled flowers, this Baron's hermit appears nearly stationary, like a graceful hovercraft.

Where do passions find room in
so diminutive a body? They often fight
with the fury of lions, until one of
the combatants falls . . .

—Hector St. John de Crevecoeur

*Not always the lightest and sweetest of birds, hummingbirds also have a
small dark side. Inquisitive hummingbirds have been known to fly up to
people and try to feed from eye-catching, red clothing. Their bravery also
allows them to take on and win against birds as large as hawks.*

To continue with some of the hummingbird's darker mystical qualities, these aggressive little birds are also forever linked with the warrior. The Aztecs said their slain warriors became hummingbirds in the afterlife, drinking nectar in the gardens of paradise, and eventually returned to earth in hummingbird form. The sun is said to shine brilliantly upon the hummingbird warriors to reward their bravery and give it beauty.

The Taino people of Florida and the Caribbean used their word for hummingbird to refer to their bravest warriors. For the Navajos, the hummingbird remains a symbol of courage, alongside the eagle and the wolf.

The Apache also have a tale about a brave warrior, Wind Dancer, who came back to earth as a hummingbird. He was brilliantly colored and painted in the same patterns as his ceremonial war paint and uniform that he wore into battle.

I am the **Shining One**, bird, warrior, and wizard.

—Aztec Chant

As if inlaid with brilliants from the mine,
or made of tearless rainbows, such as span
the unclouded skies of Peristan.

—William Hazlitt

Some tribes, such as the Hopi and Zuni, believed that hummingbirds, not being gods, ancestors, or warriors, were responsible for persuading the gods to bring rain. Pueblo Indians had dance rituals while wearing hummingbird feathers that were supposed to bring downpours to the land. Such tribes never tampered with a hummer nest for fear of causing a flood.

The most delightful legend related to rain also comes from the Pueblo, in which the hummingbird obtained its brilliantly colored gorget by flying through a rainbow while in search of rain.

This fiery-throated hummingbird is stealing a taste from a heliconia in the Costa Rican cloudforest. He is marked by a white spot behind the eye and a brilliant orange and yellow gorget that glistens like a rainbow in the sunlight.

The black-bellied hummingbird flies in for nectar, spreading its starkly contrasting white and black tail feathers.

With their amazing appearance, abilities, and acrobatics, it's easy to understand how such an incredible creature could inspire so many cultures and various legends, myths, and tales. Unlike any other bird in the world, these wonders of the sky are truly enchanting, and their presence throughout the millennia has garnered a huge fan base and plenty of mystery for the special powers these brave birds possess. Little may be known about their actual evolution, but however the hummingbird was made, and whatever gifts it may be able to bring into our lives, the miracle of the hummingbird is one that will captivate and amaze science, poets, storytellers, gardeners, and birdwatchers for the foreseeable future.

Voyager on golden air,

Type of all that's fleet and fair,

Incarnate gem,

Live diadem

Bird-beam of the summer day,

Whither on your summer way.

—John Vance Cheney

These ruby-throated hummingbirds hover beside a red and yellow flower. The males have a red gorget that glistens like rubies in the sun. The females and young males have less color on the sides, white bellies, and white throats. The two are either in a territory dispute or are about to start a courtship ritual.

A male green-crowned brilliant hummingbird feeds from a bromeliad in a Costa Rican cloudforest. Note the solid green body and crown, tiny white spot behind the eye, and forked tail. The female looks almost the same as the male except for her white breast speckled with green.

Photography Credits